D0594346

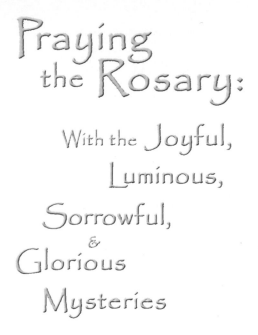

Praying the Rosary:

With the Joyful, Luminous, Sorrowful, & Glorious Mysteries

Michael Dubruiel & Amy Welborn

OUR SUNDAY VISITOR PUBLISHING DIVISION
OUR SUNDAY VISITOR, INC.
HUNTINGTON, INDIANA 46750

Nihil Obstat: Rev. Michael Heintz
Censor Librorum

Imprimatur: ✠ John M. D'Arcy
Bishop of Fort Wayne-South Bend
May 1, 2003
Feast of St. Joseph the Worker

The *nihil obstat* and *imprimatur* are declarations that a work is free from
doctrinal or moral error. It is not implied that those who have granted the *nihil
obstat* and *imprimatur* agree with the contents, opinions,
or statements expressed.

Our Sunday Visitor Publishing Division
Our Sunday Visitor, Inc.
200 Noll Plaza
Huntington, IN 46750

ISBN: 1-978-59276-151-7 (Inventory No. T202)

LCCN: 2003106659

Cover design by Troy Lefevra

Cover icon "Mother of God Enthroned With Christ Child,"
courtesy St. Isaac of Syria Skete.

Interior design by Sherri L. Hoffman

Interior icons courtesy St. Isaac of Syria Skete. To obtain any
of the icons individually, go to *www.skete.com*.

PRINTED IN CANADA

To the Patroness of the United States:
the Blessed Virgin Mary
Immaculately Conceived.
In this Year of the Rosary
October 2002-2003

O Mary, pray for us, that we may be made worthy
of the promises of Christ!

"All of Creation," St. Catherine's Monastery

Contents

Introduction

To recite the Rosary is nothing other than to contemplate with Mary the face of Christ.

POPE JOHN PAUL II
(*ROSARIUM VIRGINIS MARIAE*, NO. 3)

The Rosary:
Way of Christian Contemplation

When Pope John Paul II released his apostolic letter on the Rosary in October 2002, he made news because in it he proposed the addition of a new set of mysteries, the Luminous or Mysteries of Light, to the traditional Joyful, Sorrowful, and Glorious mysteries of the Rosary. But the Holy Father did much more than this in his letter: he also called for a renewal of this devotion, which he described as the "most effective means" of fostering contemplation on the mystery of Christ.

At the heart of the Rosary prayer is the meditation of the mysteries of our salvation wrought by Christ our Lord. The repetitive praying of Hail Marys accompanies our requests that the Blessed Virgin Mary intercede for us so that we might be

formed into perfect disciples of her Son. Th[e]
says, "To look upon the face of Christ, to recog[nize]
its mystery amid the daily events and the suffering
of his human life, and then to grasp the divine splen-
dor definitively revealed in the Risen Lord, seated in
glory at the right hand of the Father: this is the task
of every follower of Christ and therefore the task of
each one of us," (*Rosarium Virginis Mariae*, no. 9)

This small book is fashioned after the manner
in which the Holy Father presented the praying of
the Rosary in his apostolic letter. May the Blessed
Virgin Mary intercede for you with her Son as you
use it as an aid in praying the Holy Rosary.

Mary: The Model of Contemplation

In his apostolic letter, John Paul II wrote that
the most important reason to encourage the practice
of the Rosary is that it fosters a "commitment to
the contemplation of the Christian mystery" in
all of its richness. Our model of contemplation,
the Pope says, is Mary. In the way that any mother
would look upon the face of her child, Mary as
the mother of Jesus is the perfect model for our
approach to contemplation of the face of Christ.

...ospels show that the gaze of Mary varied ...nding upon the circumstances of life. So it ...ll be with us. Each time we pick up the holy beads to recite the Rosary, our gaze at the mystery of Christ will differ depending on where we find ourselves at that moment.

Thereafter Mary's gaze, ever filled with adoration and wonder, would never leave him. At times it would be *a questioning look*, as in the episode of the finding in the Temple: "Son, why have you treated us so?" (Lk 2:48); it would always be *a penetrating gaze*, one capable of deeply understanding Jesus, even to the point of perceiving his hidden feelings and anticipating his decisions, as at Cana (cf. Jn 2:5). At other times it would be *a look of sorrow*, especially beneath the Cross, where her vision would still be that of a mother giving birth, for Mary not only shared the passion and death of her Son, she also received the new son given to her in the beloved disciple (cf. Jn 19:26-27). On the morning of Easter hers would be *a gaze radiant with the joy of the Resurrection*, and finally, on the day of Pentecost, *a gaze afire* with the outpouring of the Spirit (cf. *Acts* 1:14) [*Rosarium Virginis Mariae*, no. 10].

As we pray the Rosary, then, we join with Mary in contemplating Christ. With her, we remember Christ, we proclaim Him, we learn from Him, and, most importantly, as we raise our voices in prayer and our hearts in contemplation of the holy mysteries, this "compendium of the Gospel" itself, we are conformed to Him.

How to Use This Book
in Prayer

The meditations in this book are presented in the
format suggested by Pope John Paul II in his apostolic letter on the Rosary, *Rosarium Virginis Mariae*.
What follows are the elements of each meditation.

Announcing the Mystery
As we pray the Rosary to join Mary in contemplation of her Son, we begin by announcing each
mystery. In doing so, we focus our attention on
this moment in the life of Christ. Using an image
like the icons provided for each mystery in this book
further helps us enter into the scenario that oc-
curred as God entered the reality of human life
through His Son.

Listening to the Word of God
We read a Scripture passage that helps, as the Holy
Father says, give "a biblical foundation and greater
depth to our meditation" on the mystery that has
just been announced. We listen to the Scripture
reading in the same spirit that we always do: with a

heart open to God speaking to us at this moment through His eternal Word.

Silence

Before proceeding with vocal prayer, we pause for a moment of silence. During this silence, we let go of the busyness of our lives and focus on the content of the mystery.

The Our Father

Through each of these mysteries, Jesus leads us to the Father, so it is natural for us to begin our vocal prayer with the Our Father. As we pray, we are joined to Jesus, who wants us to share in His intimacy with the Father.

The Ten Hail Marys

The prayer that we offer to Mary is rooted in and ultimately reflective of the love God has for us. The first part of the prayer is drawn from Scripture: from the words that the angel says to Mary at the Annunciation and the words of Elizabeth's greeting at the Visitation. The "center of gravity" of the prayer is the name of Jesus, the name that gives meaning to what comes before and after it. Pope

Paul VI drew attention to the custom of adding a phrase specific to the mystery being contemplated after the name of Jesus, a suggestion we have incorporated into this book.

The 'Gloria' (or the Glory Be)

The contemplation of each mystery culminates with the prayer giving glory to the three Divine Persons of the Holy Trinity. The prayers we have offered during each decade are enlivened by the love of Christ and of Mary, and raise us to the heights of heaven and the glory God has promised.

The Concluding Short Prayer

A traditional prayer that concludes each decade asks that we might "imitate what they contain and obtain what they promise." In his apostolic letter, the Holy Father suggests that each mystery might conclude with a prayer for just that intention, but one "for the fruits specific to that particular mystery." In this book, the prayers concluding each decade are offered in that spirit.

Fruit of Praying the Rosary

Praying the Rosary and meditating on the mysteries of the life of Our Lord should bear great fruit in our spiritual lives. As Pope John Paul II said in his encyclical on the Eucharist, *Ecclesia de Eucharistia*:

> To contemplate the face of Christ, and to contemplate it with Mary, is the "program" which I have set before the Church at the dawn of the third millennium, summoning her to put out into the deep on the sea of history with the enthusiasm of the new evangelization. To contemplate Christ involves being able to recognize him wherever he manifests himself, in his many forms of presence, but above all in the living sacrament of his body and his blood [no. 6].

If we faithfully commit ourselves to the Holy Rosary of the Blessed Virgin Mary, we will find that we begin to recognize Christ in the many ways He is made present to us every day. We will see that the mysteries of His life continue to unfold in His mysterious workings in our daily lives.

May the Blessed Mother of our Lord Jesus Christ intercede for you, that you might truly contemplate the face of Christ and "recognize him wherever he manifests himself" in your life!

THE JOYFUL MYSTERIES
(Prayed on Mondays and Saturdays)

The first five decades, the "joyful mysteries," are marked by *the joy radiating from the event of the Incarnation.* . . . To meditate upon the "joyful" mysteries, then, is to enter into the ultimate causes and the deepest meaning of Christian joy. It is to focus on the realism of the mystery of the Incarnation and on the obscure foreshadowing of the mystery of the saving Passion. Mary leads us to discover the secret of Christian joy, reminding us that Christianity is, first and foremost, *euanggelion,* "good news," which has as its heart and its whole content the person of Jesus Christ, the Word made flesh, the one Savior of the world.

POPE JOHN PAUL II
(*ROSARIUM VIRGINIS MARIAE*, NO. 20)

+ The Annunciation to Mary
+ The Visitation of Mary
+ The Nativity of Our Lord
+ The Presentation of the Lord
+ The Finding in the Temple

The First Joyful Mystery

The Annunciation to Mary

"Annunciation of the Mother of God," Dionysiou Monastery

In the sixth month the angel Gabriel was sent from God to a city of Galilee named Nazareth, to a virgin betrothed to a man whose name was Joseph, of the house of David; and the virgin's name was Mary. And he came to her and said, "Hail, full of grace, the Lord is with you!"

LUKE 1:26–28

The angel's greeting to Mary is one of joy as the hoped-for Messiah's coming is announced. Ask Our Lady to help you pray this decade, pondering the joy of God coming to save His people.

Silence

- *Our Father*
- *10 Hail Marys*
- *Optional prayer added to each Hail Mary:* ". . . Blessed is the fruit of thy womb, Jesus, **who came to save us**."
- *Glory Be*
- *Optional Fátima Prayer:* "O my Jesus . . ." (See page 63 for the complete text.)

Lord, through the meditation of this mystery of the Holy Rosary, reveal to us the joy you give when we say yes to all you ask of us.

The Second Joyful Mystery

The Visitation of Mary

"Mother of God of Yaroslavi"

Elizabeth was filled with the Holy Spirit and she exclaimed with a loud cry, "Blessed are you among women, and blessed is the fruit of your womb! And why is this granted me, that the mother of my Lord should come to me? For behold, when the voice of your greeting came to my ears, the babe in my womb leaped for joy."

LUKE 1:41–44

The presence of Christ within Mary brings great joy to John the Baptist, still within Elizabeth's womb. Ask Our Lady to help you pray this decade, pondering the joy that Our Lord brings to His people from the first moment of His conception.

Silence

- *Our Father*
- *10 Hail Marys*
- *Optional prayer added to each Hail Mary:* ". . . Blessed is the fruit of thy womb, Jesus, **who brings joy to his people**."
- *Glory Be*
- *Optional Fátima Prayer:* "O my Jesus . . ."

Lord, through the meditation of this mystery of the Holy Rosary, reveal to us the joy that comes when we recognize your presence in our midst.

The Third Joyful Mystery

The Nativity of Our Lord

"Nativity of Christ," Stavronikita Monastery

And the angel said to them, "Be not afraid; for behold, I bring you good news of a great joy which will come to all the people; for to you is born this day in the city of David a Savior, who is Christ the Lord. And this will be a sign for you: you will find a babe wrapped in swaddling cloths and lying in a manger."

LUKE 2:10–12

The angels announce the message that dispels the fears of the ages and joyfully fulfills our hopes. Ask Our Lady to help you pray this decade, pondering the joy of the great miracle of the Word made flesh.

Silence

- *Our Father*
- *10 Hail Marys*
- *Optional prayer added to each Hail Mary:* ". . . Blessed is the fruit of thy womb, Jesus, **who was born to save us.**"
- *Glory Be*
- *Optional Fátima Prayer:* "O my Jesus . . ."

Lord, through the meditation of this mystery of the Holy Rosary, reveal to us the joy that Jesus' birth brings to a fearful world.

The Fourth Joyful Mystery

The Presentation of the Lord

"Presentation in the Temple," Dionysiou Monastery

[Simeon] took him up in his arms and blessed God .. said, "Lord, now lettest thou thy servant depart in peace according to thy word; for mine eyes have seen thy salvation which thou hast prepared in the presence of all peoples, a light for revelation to the Gentiles, and for glory to thy people Israel."

LUKE 2:28–32

Simeon longed for the coming of the Messiah, whom God had promised he would see before he died. Ask Our Lady to help you pray this decade, pondering the joy felt by all people of goodwill at the coming of the Lord.

Silence

- *Our Father*
- *10 Hail Marys*
- *Optional prayer added to each Hail Mary:* ". . . Blessed is the fruit of thy womb, Jesus, **who was presented in the Temple**."
- *Glory Be*
- *Optional Fátima Prayer:* "O my Jesus . . ."

Lord, through the meditation of this mystery of the Holy Rosary, reveal to us the joy of those who hold to your word with faith that it will be fulfilled.

The Fifth Joyful Mystery

The Finding in the Temple

"Christ in the Temple at Age Twelve," Novgorod

After three days they found him in the temple, sitting among the teachers, listening to them and asking them questions; and all who heard him were amazed at his understanding and his answers. And when they saw him they were astonished; and his mother said to him, "Son, why have you treated us so? Behold, your father and I have been looking for you anxiously." And he said to them, "How is it that you sought me? Did you not know that I must be in my Father's house?"

LUKE 2:46–49

Joseph and Mary lost their young son. Now, after three days, they joyfully find Him. Ask Our Lady to help you pray this decade, pondering the joy that she felt when she first caught sight of her son.

Silence

- *Our Father*
- *10 Hail Marys*
- *Optional prayer added to each Hail Mary:* ". . . Blessed is the fruit of thy womb, Jesus, *who was found in the Temple*."
- *Glory Be*
- *Optional Fátima Prayer:* "O my Jesus . . ."

Lord, through the meditation of this mystery of the Holy Rosary, reveal to us the joy of those who search for and find you.

THE LUMINOUS
MYSTERIES

(Prayed on Thursdays)

It is during the years of his public ministry that *the mystery of Christ is most evidently a mystery of light*: "While I am in the world, I am the light of the world" (Jn 9:5). . . .
Each of these mysteries is a revelation of the Kingdom now present in the very person of Jesus.

POPE JOHN PAUL II
(*ROSARIUM VIRGINIS MARIAE*, NOS. 19 AND 21)

✦ The Baptism of the Lord
✦ The Wedding Feast at Cana
✦ The Preaching of the Kingdom of God
✦ The Transfiguration of the Lord
✦ The Institution of the Eucharist

The First Luminous Mystery
The Baptism of the Lord

"Theophany of the Lord," Dionysiou Monastery

*And when Jesus was baptized, he went up immediately
from the water, and behold, the heavens were opened and
he saw the Spirit of God descending like a dove, and alight-
ing on him; and lo, a voice from heaven, saying, "This is
my beloved Son, with whom I am well pleased."*

MATTHEW 3:16–17

Our Lord, though innocent, takes on our sins as
He enters the water of the Jordan and is baptized by
John. His mission of our salvation is blessed by the
Father's praise and the Spirit's descent. Ask Our Lady
to help you pray this decade, pondering the light
that comes from submission to the will of God.

Silence

- *Our Father*
- *10 Hail Marys*
- *Optional prayer added to each Hail Mary:*
  ". . . Blessed is the fruit of thy womb, Jesus, **who
  was baptized by John in the Jordan**.
- *Glory Be*
- *Optional Fátima Prayer:* "O my Jesus . . ."

Lord, through the meditation of this mystery of
the Holy Rosary, reveal to us the light that was
given to us in baptism.

The Second Luminous Mystery

The Wedding Feast at Cana

"Christ Changing Water to Wine," Decani Monastery

*When the wine failed, the mother of Jesus said to him,
"They have no wine." And Jesus said to her, "O woman,
what have you to do with me? My hour has not yet come."
His mother said to the servants, "Do whatever he tells
you."*

JOHN 2:3–5

Our Lord works His first miracle at the request of
His mother, who proclaims her belief that He can
do all things. Ask Our Lady to help you pray this
decade, pondering the light of living in confidence
that Jesus can fulfill all our needs.

Silence

- *Our Father*
- *10 Hail Marys*
- *Optional prayer added to each Hail Mary:*
  ". . . Blessed is the fruit of thy womb, Jesus, **who
  changed the water into wine**."
- *Glory Be*
- *Optional Fátima Prayer:* "O my Jesus . . ."

Lord, through the meditation of this mystery of
the Holy Rosary, reveal to us the light that comes
when we turn to you for our every need.

The Third Luminous Mystery

The Preaching of the Kingdom of God

"Raising of Lazarus," Dionysiou Monastery

Jesus came into Galilee, preaching the gospel of God, and saying, "The time is fulfilled, and the kingdom of God is at hand; repent, and believe in the gospel."

MARK 1:14–15

Our Lord invites us to become subjects of the Kingdom of God by turning from our sins and trusting in the life-giving message of the Gospel. Ask Our Lady to help you pray this decade to live in the light of discipleship.

Silence

- *Our Father*
- *10 Hail Marys*
- *Optional prayer added to each Hail Mary:* ". . . Blessed is the fruit of thy womb, Jesus, *who invites us to seek the reign of God in our lives.*"
- *Glory Be*
- *Optional Fátima Prayer:* "O my Jesus . . ."

Lord, through the meditation of this mystery of the Holy Rosary, reveal to us the light that comes when we seek first the Kingdom of God.

The Fourth Luminous Mystery

The Transfiguration of the Lord

"Transfiguration of the Lord," Dionysiou Monastery

Peter said to Jesus, "Master, it is well that we are here; let us make three booths, one for you and one for Moses and one for Elijah" — not knowing what he said. As he said this, a cloud came and overshadowed them; and they were afraid as they entered the cloud. And a voice came out of the cloud, saying, "This is my Son, my Chosen; listen to him!" And when the voice had spoken, Jesus was found alone.

LUKE 9:33–36

The apostles witness that transfiguration of the Lord and hear the voice of the Father commanding them to listen to Jesus. Ask Our Lady to help you pray this decade to see the light that always lies ahead for the follower of Christ no matter how dark the present may appear.

Silence

- *Our Father*
- *10 Hail Marys*
- *Optional prayer added to each Hail Mary:* ". . . Blessed is the fruit of thy womb, Jesus, **who was transfigured before the apostles' eyes**."
- *Glory Be*
- *Optional Fátima Prayer:* "O my Jesus . . ."

Lord, through the meditation of this mystery of the Holy Rosary, reveal to us the light that awaits those who listen to your Son and follow him faithfully.

The Fifth Luminous Mystery

The Institution of the Eucharist

"Mystical Supper," Vatopedi Monastery

Now as they were eating, Jesus took bread, and blessed, and broke it, and gave it to the disciples and said, "Take, eat; this is my body." And he took a cup, and when he had given thanks he gave it to them, saying, "Drink of it, all of you; for this is my blood of the covenant, which is poured out for many for the forgiveness of sins."

MATTHEW 26:26–28

At the Last Supper, the Lord reveals to His disciples that He will suffer and die for our salvation. Ask Our Lady to help you pray this decade to know the love of Our Lord made manifest in His passion and in His abiding presence in the Blessed Sacrament.

Silence

- *Our Father*
- *10 Hail Marys*
- *Optional prayer added to each Hail Mary:* ". . . Blessed is the fruit of thy womb, Jesus, **who gives himself to us in the Eucharist.**"
- *Glory Be*
- *Optional Fátima Prayer:* "O my Jesus . . ."

Lord, through the meditation of this mystery of the Holy Rosary, reveal to us the light that comes when we receive the Body and Blood of your Son in the Eucharist.

THE SORROWFUL MYSTERIES

(Prayed on Tuesdays and Fridays)

The Gospels give great prominence to the sorrowful mysteries of Christ. From the beginning Christian piety, especially during the Lenten devotion of the Way of the Cross, has focused on the individual moments of the Passion, realizing that here is found the culmination of the revelation of God's love and the source of our salvation. The Rosary selects certain moments from the Passion, inviting the faithful to contemplate them in their hearts and to relive them. . . . The sorrowful mysteries help the believer to relive the death of Jesus, to stand at the foot of the Cross beside Mary, to enter with her into the depths of God's love for man and to experience all its life–giving power.

POPE JOHN PAUL II
(*ROSARIUM VIRGINIS MARIAE*, NO. 22)

✦ **The Agony in the Garden**

✦ **The Scourging at the Pillar**

✦ **The Crowning With Thorns**

✦ **The Carrying of the Cross**

✦ **The Crucifixion of Our Lord**

The First Sorrowful Mystery

The Agony in the Garden

"Gethsemane," St. Clement's Church, Macedonia

And when he came to the place he said to them, "Pray that you may not enter into temptation." And he withdrew from them about a stone's throw, and knelt down and prayed, "Father, if thou art willing, remove this cup from me; nevertheless not my will, but thine, be done."

LUKE 22:40–42

In the garden of Gethsemane, Our Lord experiences the weight of humanity's temptations and sins, yet in His agony He prays that God's will be done. Ask Our Lady to help you pray this decade to experience the sorrow of the suffering Jesus and to "watch" with Him in His agony.

Silence

- *Our Father*
- *10 Hail Marys*
- *Optional prayer added to each Hail Mary:* ". . . Blessed is the fruit of thy womb, Jesus, **who prayed that the Father's will be done**.
- *Glory Be*
- *Optional Fátima Prayer:* "O my Jesus . . ."

Lord, through the meditation of this mystery of the Holy Rosary, help us feel sorrow for what we add to your Son's agony when we do not pray.

The Second Sorrowful Mystery

The Scourging at the Pillar

"Scourging," Stavronikita Monastery

Then Pilate took Jesus and scourged him.

JOHN 19:1

The path of faithfulness to the will of the Father is difficult. Our Lord is scourged at the pillar and endures horrible torture out of love for us. Ask Our Lady to help you pray this decade to experience sorrow for your sins that cause the Lord to suffer so greatly.

Silence

- *Our Father*
- *10 Hail Marys*
- *Optional prayer added to each Hail Mary:* ". . . Blessed is the fruit of thy womb, Jesus, *who was scourged for our sins.*"
- *Glory Be*
- *Optional Fátima Prayer:* "O my Jesus . . ."

Lord, through the meditation of this mystery of the Holy Rosary, lead us to experience greater sorrow for the suffering our inaction brings to others.

The Third Sorrowful Mystery

The Crowning With Thorns

"Bridegroom," Lionda

Then the soldiers of the governor took Jesus into the prae-torium, and they gathered the whole battalion before him. And they stripped him and put a scarlet robe upon him, and plaiting a crown of thorns they put it on his head, and put a reed in his right hand. And kneeling before him they mocked him, saying, "Hail, King of the Jews!"

MATTHEW 27:27–29

Jesus is mocked as a king because His followers have abandoned Him. Ask Our Lady to help you pray this decade to experience sorrow that your King is treated so harshly.

Silence

- *Our Father*
- *10 Hail Marys*
- *Optional prayer added to each Hail Mary:* ". . . Blessed is the fruit of thy womb, Jesus, *who was mocked and crowned with thorns*."
- *Glory Be*
- *Optional Fátima Prayer:* "O my Jesus . . ."

Lord, through the meditation of this mystery of the Holy Rosary, help us experience sorrow for the times that we do not obey Christ and mock his Kingship in our lives.

The Fourth Sorrowful Mystery

The Carrying of the Cross

"Road to Calvary," Great Meteoron Monastery

And as they led him away, they seized one Simon of Cyrene, who was coming in from the country, and laid on him the cross, to carry it behind Jesus. And there followed him a great multitude of the people, and of women who bewailed and lamented him. But Jesus turning to them said, "Daughters of Jerusalem, do not weep for me, but weep for yourselves and for your children."

LUKE 23:26–28

Jesus takes a moment on His journey to Calvary to teach the women who weep for Him. He tells them to be sorrowful about their own plight. Ask Our Lady to help you as you pray this decade to feel sorrow for your sins.

Silence

- *Our Father*
- *10 Hail Marys*
- *Optional prayer added to each Hail Mary:* ". . . Blessed is the fruit of thy womb, Jesus, **who carries his cross**."
- *Glory Be*
- *Optional Fátima Prayer:* "O my Jesus . . ."

Lord, through the meditation of this mystery of the Holy Rosary, help us experience the sorrow that our sins bring to others.

The Fifth Sorrowful Mystery

The Crucifixion of Our Lord

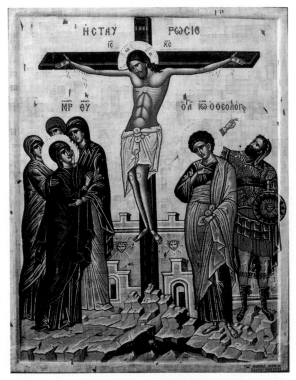

"Crucifixion," Monk Michael

When Jesus saw his mother, and the disciple whom he loved standing near, he said to his mother, "Woman, behold, your son!" Then he said to the disciple, "Behold, your mother!" And from that hour the disciple took her to his own home. After this Jesus, knowing that all was finished, . . . said, "It is finished"; and he bowed his head and gave up his spirit.

JOHN 19:26–28, 30

The disciple whom Jesus loves is you and I. Ask Our Lady to let you experience the sorrow that she felt as she watched her only Son give His life for our salvation, and beg her to be a mother to you.

Silence

- *Our Father*
- *10 Hail Marys*
- *Optional prayer added to each Hail Mary:* ". . . Blessed is the fruit of thy womb, Jesus, *who died for us on the cross.*"
- *Glory Be*
- *Optional Fátima Prayer:* "O my Jesus . . ."

Lord, through the meditation of this mystery of the Holy Rosary, help us to experience sorrow and contrition for our sins while trusting in your Divine Mercy.

THE GLORIOUS MYSTERIES

(Prayed on Wednesdays and Sundays)

The glorious mysteries thus lead the faithful to greater hope for the eschatological goal towards which they journey as members of the pilgrim People of God in history. This can only impel them to bear courageous witness to that "good news" which gives meaning to their entire existence.

POPE JOHN PAUL II
(*ROSARIUM VIRGINIS MARIAE*, NO. 23)

+ **The Resurrection of Our Lord**
+ **The Ascension of Our Lord**
+ **The Descent of the Holy Spirit**
+ **The Assumption of the Blessed Virgin**
+ **The Coronation of Mary as Queen of Heaven**

The First Glorious Mystery

The Resurrection of Our Lord

"Resurrection," Dionysiou Monastery

Simon Peter came . . . and went into the tomb; he saw the linen cloths lying, and the napkin, which had been on his head, not lying with the linen cloths but rolled up in a place by itself. Then the other disciple, who reached the tomb first, also went in, and he saw and believed; for as yet they did not know the scripture, that he must rise from the dead.

JOHN 20:6–9

The disciple whom Jesus loves peers into the empty tomb and believes. Ask Our Lady to help you as you pray this decade to experience the hope of those who believe in her Son's glorious resurrection.

Silence

- *Our Father*
- *10 Hail Marys*
- *Optional prayer added to each Hail Mary:* ". . . Blessed is the fruit of thy womb, Jesus, **who rose from the dead on the third day.**"
- *Glory Be*
- *Optional Fátima Prayer:* "O my Jesus . . ."

Lord, through the meditation of this mystery of the Holy Rosary, reveal to us the glory of the resurrection of your Son.

The Second Glorious Mystery

The Ascension of Our Lord

"Ascension of the Lord," Dionysiou Monastery

As they were looking on, he was lifted up, and a cloud took him out of their sight. And while they were gazing into heaven as he went, behold, two men stood by them in white robes, and said, "Men of Galilee, why do you stand looking into heaven? This Jesus, who was taken up from you into heaven, will come in the same way as you saw him go into heaven."

ACTS 1:9–11

The ascension of Our Lord into heaven leaves the apostles looking upward, but the angel tells them the Lord will return. Ask Our Lady to help you as you pray this decade to experience the triumph of the Lord's ascension and the glorious hope of His return.

Silence

- *Our Father*
- *10 Hail Marys*
- *Optional prayer added to each Hail Mary: ". . . Blessed is the fruit of thy womb, Jesus, **who ascended into heaven**."*
- *Glory Be*
- *Optional Fátima Prayer: "O my Jesus . . ."*

Lord, through the meditation of this mystery of the Holy Rosary, reveal to us the glory of your Son's ascension to your right hand as we seek to do your will here.

The Third Glorious Mystery

The Descent of the Holy Spirit

"*Pentecost,*" *Dionysiou Monastery*

Suddenly a sound came from heaven like the rush of a mighty wind, and it filled all the house where they were sitting. And there appeared to them tongues as of fire, distributed and resting on each one of them. And they were all filled with the Holy Spirit and began to speak in other tongues, as the Spirit gave them utterance.

ACTS 2:2–4

The apostles were instructed by Our Lord to await the coming of the Holy Spirit in Jerusalem. They fulfill their mission from the Lord and are blessed with the coming of the Spirit. Ask Our Lady to help you as you pray this decade to experience the empowering presence of the Holy Spirit.

Silence

- *Our Father*
- *10 Hail Marys*
- *Optional prayer added to each Hail Mary:* ". . . Blessed is the fruit of thy womb, Jesus, *who promised the Holy Spirit to his Church*."
- *Glory Be*
- *Optional Fátima Prayer:* "O my Jesus . . ."

Lord, through the meditation of this mystery of the Holy Rosary, reveal to us the glory of the presence of the Spirit that empowers us to fulfill your will.

The Fourth Glorious Mystery

The Assumption of the Blessed Virgin

"Dormition of the Mother of God," Dionysiou Monastery

The princess is decked in her chamber with gold-woven robes; in many-colored robes she is led to the king, with her virgin companions, her escort, in her train. With joy and gladness they are led along as they enter the palace of the king.

PSALM 45:13–15

Jesus had promised that whoever believed in Him would share in His resurrection. Our Lady is the first believer and the first to experience the fruits of His redemption, both in her immaculate conception and now in her glorious assumption. Ask Our Lady to help you as you pray this decade to believe as she did.

Silence

- *Our Father*
- *10 Hail Marys*
- *Optional prayer added to each Hail Mary:* "... Blessed is the fruit of thy womb, Jesus, ***who has brought his mother into heaven.***"
- *Glory Be*
- *Optional Fátima Prayer:* "O my Jesus ..."

Lord, through the meditation of this mystery of the Holy Rosary, reveal to us the glory that awaits all who share in the redemption of your Son.

The Fifth Glorious Mystery

The Coronation of Mary as Queen of Heaven

"Mother of God Enthroned With Christ Child"

A great portent appeared in heaven, a woman clothed with the sun, with the moon under her feet, and on her head a crown of twelve stars.

REVELATION 12:1

Mary is crowned Queen of Heaven and Earth. She is the mother of the Church. Ask Our Lady to help you as you pray this decade to enjoy her glorious intercession for all of your needs here on this earth.

Silence

- *Our Father*
- *10 Hail Marys*
- *Optional prayer added to each Hail Mary:* ". . . Blessed is the fruit of thy womb, Jesus, **who crowned his mother Queen of Heaven and Earth.**
- *Glory Be*
- *Optional Fátima Prayer:* "O my Jesus . . ."

Lord, through the meditation of this mystery of the Holy Rosary, reveal to us the glorious hope that is ours in having as an intercessor the Queen of Heaven and Earth, the mother of your Son.

Rosary Prayers

Sign of the Cross

In the name of the Father, and of the Son, and of the Holy Spirit. Amen.

Apostles' Creed

I believe in God, the Father almighty, creator of heaven and earth; and in Jesus Christ, his only Son, our Lord; who was conceived by the Holy Spirit, born of the Virgin Mary, suffered under Pontius Pilate, was crucified, died, and was buried. He descended to the dead; the third day he arose again from the dead. He ascended into heaven and sits at the right hand of God, the Father almighty; from thence he shall come to judge the living and the dead. I believe in the Holy Spirit, the holy catholic Church, the communion of saints, the forgiveness of sins, the resurrection of the body, and life everlasting. Amen.

Our Father

Our Father, who art in heaven, hallowed be thy name. Thy kingdom come. Thy will be done on earth, as it is in heaven. Give us this day our daily bread, and forgive us our trespasses, as we forgive those who trespass against us, and lead us not into temptation, but deliver us from evil. Amen.

Hail Mary
Hail Mary, full of grace. The Lord is with thee. Blessed art thou among women, and blessed is the fruit of thy womb, Jesus. Holy Mary, Mother of God, pray for us sinners, now and at the hour of our death. Amen.

Glory Be
Glory be to the Father, and to the Son, and to the Holy Spirit. As it was in the beginning, is now, and ever shall be, world without end. Amen.

Fátima Prayer
O my Jesus, forgive us our sins, save us from the fires of hell, lead all souls to heaven, especially those who have most need of your mercy. Amen.

Hail, Holy Queen
Hail, holy Queen, Mother of Mercy, our life, our sweetness, and our hope. To thee do we cry, poor

banished children of Eve; to thee do we send up our sighs, mourning, and weeping in this valley of tears. Turn then, most gracious advocate, thine eyes of mercy toward us, and after this, our exile, show unto us the blessed fruit of thy womb, Jesus. O clement, O loving, O sweet Virgin Mary.

V. Pray for us, O Holy Mother of God.
R. That we may be made worthy of the promises of Christ.

Concluding Rosary Prayer

Let us pray: O God, whose only begotten Son, by his life, death, and resurrection, has purchased for us the rewards of eternal life, grant, we beseech thee, that meditating upon these mysteries of the Most Holy Rosary of the Blessed Virgin Mary, we may imitate what they contain and obtain what they promise, through the same Christ our Lord. Amen.